M000096998

The Process of Biblical Change

by

Julie Ganschow

MABC, Certified Biblical Counselor

THE PROCESS OF BIBLICAL CHANGE
Copyright © 2009
Second Edition 2017
Published by Pure Water Press, Kansas City, Missouri
Web: www.rgcconline.org
Web: www.biblicalcounselingforwomen.org
Blog: bc4women.blogspot.com
Email : reigninggracecounsel@rgcconline.org

Printed in the United States of America.

ISBN-13: 978-0615809045 (Pure Water Press)
ISBN-10:0615809049

Dedication

In the counseling room, nothing is more important than imparting to the counselee the necessity of heart change. In my ministry I have often desired to have the printed word to hand my counselees to reinforce the content of the counseling session regarding the process of mind renewal. What you hold in your hand is the result of this desire. It came about as a result of speaking to my own son about the process of biblical change in his life, and it is to him I dedicate this little booklet for the glory of God.

Dear Beloved Counselee,

You are looking for counsel because of a problem in your life. You may have a marriage that is in distress, an eating disorder, sinful anger, depression, anxiety, feelings of being unhappy. Maybe you have relationship problems, drug or alcohol abuse, struggles with immorality, or a host of other possibilities. Perhaps you have had previous counseling for this same issue. You may have come with a basket of issues that you would like to resolve or gain control of. Most people come for counseling expecting to deal with one or two specific things.

You come with the thought (expectation?) that you will talk about the problem, the counselor will listen and this will somehow make things better in your life. This has not proven to be an effective method of bringing about real and lasting change.

What you are about to embark on here is a process. It is the process of biblical change. This change began at your salvation (assuming you know Jesus Christ as your Savior) and will continue until you die when you will be made perfect in all respects. It is a process of leaving behind who you were (Philippians 3:12-14), and revealing Christ in you, the hope of glory. Because it is a process geared toward change, there will be work involved–some practical homework and much more internal working.

My prayer for you is that you grasp the vital importance of biblical change and begin to live your life for the purpose of glorifying God.

> *You were taught, with regard to your former way of life, to put off your old self, which is being corrupted by its deceitful desires; to be made new in the attitude of your minds; and to put on the new self, created to be like God in true righteousness and holiness.*
>
> –Ephesians 4:22-24 (NIV)

Topics Covered

I.
Change requires an understanding of your present heart condition.

II.
There must be a desire to change to glorify God before the changes will be biblical.

III.
Inner Man/Inner Life

IV.
Change is a battle for the mind that is fought in the body.

What is the "heart"?

Definition: The heart is the biblical word used to describe the inner man. The heart is the immaterial (non-flesh) part of you that includes your thoughts, beliefs, desires, mind, feelings, intentions, and emotions. It is often referred to as the control center of your being.

We are made of essentially two parts:

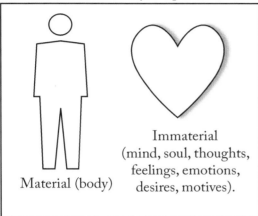

Material (body)

Immaterial (mind, soul, thoughts, feelings, emotions, desires, motives).

What you think, believe and desire in your immaterial part (mind, heart, soul, feelings), is what your material part (body) does. For example, if you think you are thirsty, you get up and get a drink. If you believe you are in danger, you run. If you desire an ice cream cone, you get one. We are used to our bodies responding to these commands automatically.

We also respond automatically to other kinds of thoughts and desires. When we become angry, we may curse or hit. When we desire escape from problems we may drink or use drugs. When we want something and don't have the money to purchase it, we may put it on credit or even steal it. When we are in trouble, we may fear exposure so we lie. These things may have become automatic for you too.

Probably without your direct knowledge, you have trained yourself to respond in a certain way when confronted by a circumstance or situation. Through repetition, it has become a habit, or pattern. These sinful patterns are found in the heart.

The Bible has much to say about the heart.

> *"As in water face reflects face, So a man's heart reveals the man."*
> Proverbs 27:19 (NKJV)

What does this mean? As water acts like a mirror and shows what you look like on the outside, your heart reflects and reveals what you are like on the inside.

"The good man brings good things out of the good stored up in his heart, and the evil man brings evil things out of the evil stored up in his heart. For out of the overflow of his heart his mouth speaks."

Luke 6:45 (NIV)

"But the things that come out of the mouth come from the heart, and these make a man 'unclean.' For out of the heart come evil thoughts, murder, adultery, sexual immorality, theft, false testimony, slander."

Matthew 15:18-19 (NIV)

Do you struggle with evil thoughts, bitterness, immorality, lying, or gossip? What does the Bible say about the condition of your heart? God's view of your heart is found in Jeremiah 17:9: "The heart is deceitful above all things, And desperately wicked; Who can know it?"

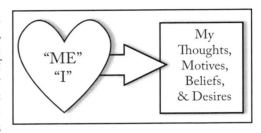

The deceitful heart is bent on satisfying *me*, having *my* own way, living life for *my* pleasures, with *me* at the center of my universe. Do these things surprise you? Because the heart has been referred to as the control center of your being, whatever you think, believe or desire in your heart is what guides and determines your actions. We do not naturally think about our heart being wicked. Many times people are referred to as having a good heart or a big heart. It is possible you have never heard someone say that your heart is deceitful and wicked and evil. Yet if you are honest with yourself, you may see that you have some of the sin habits found in Matthew 15:18-19.

Look at this passage for insight into what God sees:

*"... And they began to **think up foolish ideas** of what God was like. The result was that their minds became dark and confused. Claiming to be wise, they became utter fools instead ...*

*So God let them go ahead and do whatever shameful things their hearts desired. As a result, they did vile and degrading things with each other's bodies. Instead of believing what they knew was the truth about God, they **deliberately chose to believe lies...***

*God abandoned them to their **shameful desires**. Even the women turned against the natural way to have sex and instead indulged in sex with each other. And the men, instead of having normal sexual relationships with women, **burned with lust** for each other. Men did shameful things with other men and, as a result, suffered within themselves the penalty they so richly deserved. When they **refused to acknowledge** God, he abandoned them to their **evil minds** and let them do things that should never be done. Their lives became full of every kind of wickedness, sin, greed, hate, envy, murder, fighting, deception,*

6

malicious behavior, and gossip. They are backstabbers, haters of God, insolent, proud, and boastful. They **are forever inventing new ways of sinning** *and are disobedient to their parents. They refuse to understand, break their promises, and* **are heartless** *and unforgiving. They are* **fully aware** *of God's death penalty for those who do these things, yet they go right ahead and do them anyway. And, worse yet, they encourage others to do them, too."*

Romans 1:21-32 (NLT; emphasis added)

The sins listed in Romans 1:21-32 are the result of sinful thoughts, beliefs, and desires. Every action began as a thought. The thought was fueled by a desire or belief. The desire or belief originated in the heart.

Jesus took the opportunity to speak to the attitudes of the heart when He was questioned by the Pharisees and His disciples about pure foods and ceremonial hand-washing. He gave this wise reply:

"Can't you see that what you eat won't defile you? Food doesn't come in contact with your heart, but only passes through the stomach and then comes out again." By saying this, Jesus showed that every kind of food is acceptable. And then he added, "It is the thought-life that defiles you. For from within, out of a person's heart, come evil thoughts, sexual immorality, theft, murder, adultery, greed, wickedness, deceit, eagerness for lustful pleasure, envy, slander, pride, and foolishness. All these vile things come from within; they are what defile you and make you unacceptable to God." Mark 7:18-23 (NLT)

The vile things that come out from you originated in your heart. Before engaging in sexual immorality, there was a desire for illicit pleasure. Before stealing something, there was a belief that you were entitled to what you wanted, and a belief that you would not get caught. Before the adulterous affair, there was the desire to "be happy," to have your needs met, to feel desired by your cohort. Before the deceit, there was a fear of being caught or exposed. Before you gossiped, you believed you had a right to share that information with someone; you wanted someone else to know.

All of your actions, including whatever it was that brought you to counseling, began as a thought, belief, or desire in your heart.

The Importance of Roots and Fruits
(Please refer to the diagram of the trees on page 8 and 9)

Have you ever enjoyed a juicy peach or a crisp apple? The quality of the fruit of a tree is determined by its root system. If the roots are given nutrient-rich fertilizer, the soil will be heavy and fertile. This makes the tree strong, yielding good fruit.

If the roots are sunk in bad soil and fertilized with poor-quality additives or none at all, the roots will have little nutrition to carry up through the trunk to the branches and leaves. The tree will be weak in quality and its fruit will be poor.

The Importance of Root Issues and Fruit Issues

BAD FRUIT: The results of what we think, desire, believe, want in our hearts.

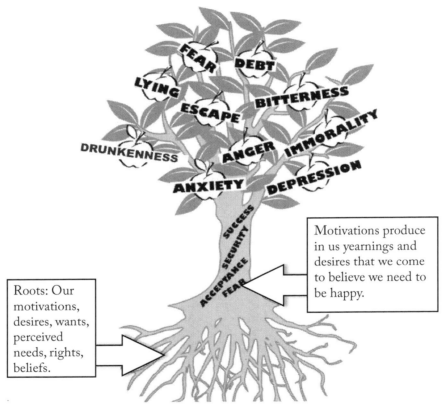

Roots: Our motivations, desires, wants, perceived needs, rights, beliefs.

Motivations produce in us yearnings and desires that we come to believe we need to be happy.

ROOTS = IDOLATROUS HEART - SELF-CENTERED

"When you follow the desires of your sinful nature, your lives will produce these evil results: sexual immorality, impure thoughts, eagerness for lustful pleasure, idolatry, participation in demonic activities, hostility, quarreling, jealousy, outbursts of anger, selfish ambition, divisions, the feeling that everyone is wrong except those in your own little group, envy, drunkenness, wild parties, and other kinds of sin."

Galations 5:19-21 (NLT)

The Importance of
Root Issues and Fruit Issues

GOOD FRUIT: The results of what we think, desire, believe, want in our hearts.

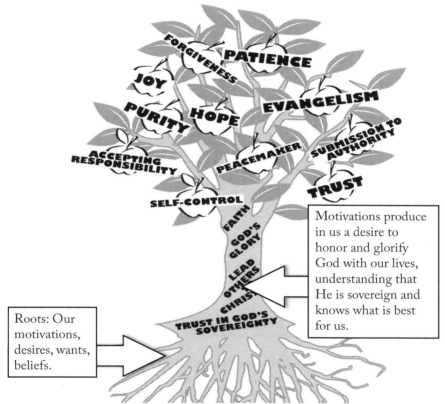

Motivations produce in us a desire to honor and glorify God with our lives, understanding that He is sovereign and knows what is best for us.

Roots: Our motivations, desires, wants, beliefs.

ROOTS = GOD CENTERED HEART DESIRE TO GLORIFY GOD.

"But when the Holy Spirit controls our lives, he will produce this kind of fruit in us: love, joy, peace, patience, kindness, goodness, faithfulness, gentleness, and self-control."
Galations 5:22-23 (NLT)

Now consider the issue(s) that brought you to counseling. Let's refer to it as fruit. In your life, you have grown some poor-quality fruit. This is a result, a product produced by something that grew it. We must conclude that a problem exists deeper down in your tree of life. Something has caused your fruit to be bad.

In the case of humanity, we can say that the root system is equal to the heart. If you have the fruit of anger, depression, anxiety, immorality, drug or alcohol abuse, lying, etc., it means that your roots are embedded in an idolatrous and self-centered heart. Your heart has been focused on your wants, perceived needs, personal rights, beliefs and desires.

Somehow you came to believe that you needed certain things or people to "make you happy." Maybe you are driven to achieve success; perhaps you desire acceptance at all costs; or maybe fear of not being accepted or secure controls you. These motivations spurred on by the desires of the heart have born exactly the kind of fruit you would expect—awful fruit. If this were not so, you would not be seeking counseling!

It is shocking to some counselees that we don't focus on the anger or the drunkenness specifically while counseling. It is not profitable to simply pull the bad fruit off the tree, because soon new bad fruit will grow in its place. The consequences you are experiencing are the *result* of the problem. They are not the problem.

We will find the problem where it really dwells, in the roots—in your heart. What is guiding and motivating your heart is what will change your actions and consequences (the fruit).

When your thoughts, beliefs and desires are set on glorifying God, there will be right actions and good consequences. But because of a heart that is set on pleasing "self," your thoughts and actions are not naturally going to be like God's. This presents a dilemma because God commands us in the Bible to be holy.

> *"But now you must be holy in everything you do, just as God – who chose you to be his children – is holy. For he himself has said, "You must be holy because I am holy."*   1 Peter 1:15-16 (NLT)

Practicing holiness brings God glory. Glorifying God is to be the goal of your life. I am often asked by my counselees, "Why am I here?" The simple and straightforward answer to this question could change your life: You are here to glorify God.

Glorifying God happens when the focus of life changes from living for my pleasure and glory to living for His pleasure and glory. It demands that my heart change from a me-centered focus to a God-centered focus.

In order to accomplish this goal, changes must take place. The first change that must take place is in the heart itself. You cannot change your own heart. Because your heart is deceitful and wicked (Jer. 17:9), you cannot possibly know the depths of its depravity, nor can you conjure up enough goodness within yourself to change in a real and lasting way. You may have tried this before through a New Year's Resolution or a "self-help" group of some kind. Your behavior may have changed for a while or to some degree, but studies bear out the fact that merely altering behavior does not bring about lasting and permanent change.

10

Only God can change the human heart.

> *"And I will give you a new heart with new and right desires, and I will put a new spirit in you. I will take out your stony heart of sin and give you a new, obedient heart."* Ezekiel 36:26 (NLT)

> *"And I will give them singleness of heart and put a new spirit within them. I will take away their hearts of stone and give them tender hearts instead, so they will obey my laws and regulations. Then they will truly be my people, and I will be their God."* Ezekiel 11:19-20 (NLT)

> *"And I will give them one heart and mind to worship me forever, for their own good and for the good of all their descendants."* Jeremiah 32:39 (NLT)

A new heart is given by God at salvation. Salvation is necessary because of sin.

> *"For all have sinned; all fall short of God's glorious standard."* Romans 3:23 (NLT)

Psalm 51 is the account of David, "a man after God's own heart," who sinned greatly in his life. Read his words below:

> *"Have mercy on me, O God, because of your unfailing love. Because of your great compassion, blot out the stain of my sins. Wash me clean from my guilt. Purify me from my sin. For I recognize my shameful deeds— they haunt me day and night. Against you, and you alone, have I sinned; I have done what is evil in your sight. You will be proved right in what you say, and your judgment against me is just. For I was born a sinner—yes, from the moment my mother conceived me. But you desire honesty from the heart, so you can teach me to be wise in my inmost being. Purify me from my sins, and I will be clean; wash me, and I will be whiter than snow."* Psalm 51:1-7 (NLT)

> *"Today you must listen to his voice. Don't harden your hearts against him as Israel did when they rebelled."*
>
> Hebrews 3:7-8 (NLT)

This wise man recognized that he was in deep trouble. He knew his sin had separated him from God. It wasn't just the sin he committed at that time, but he admits he "was born a sinner." He understood there would be judgment for his sin and he asked for pardon from his sins, for redemption, salvation. First Corinthians 6:9-10 tell us that because of their sin, the unsaved will not inherit the kingdom of God.

11

"Do you not know that the wicked will not inherit the kingdom of God? Do not be deceived: Neither the sexually immoral nor idolaters nor adulterers nor male prostitutes nor homosexual offenders nor thieves nor the greedy nor drunkards nor slanderers nor swindlers will inherit the kingdom of God."

I Corinthians 6:9-10 (NIV)

"But the cowardly, the unbelieving, the vile, the murderers, the sexually immoral, those who practice magic arts, the idolaters and all liars—their place will be in the fiery lake of burning sulfur. This is the second death."

Revelation 21:8 (NIV)

To not "inherit the kingdom of God" means that you will be eternally separated from Him. When you take your last breath, you will be lost and without hope for all eternity. There will be no second chance or reprieve.

Perhaps you have heard this before and discounted it. God urged His people over and over, but some did not heed His call.

"But no, you won't listen. So you are storing up terrible punishment for yourself because of your stubbornness in refusing to turn from your sin. For there is going to come a day of judgment when God, the just judge of all the world, will judge all people according to what they have done. He will give eternal life to those who persist in doing what is good, seeking after the glory and honor and immortality that God offers. But he will pour out his anger and wrath on those who live for themselves, who refuse to obey the truth and practice evil deeds."

Romans 2:5-8 (NLT)

"For the wages of sin is death, but the gift of God is eternal life in Christ Jesus our Lord."   Romans 6:23 (NIV)

The good news is that Jesus Christ came to redeem sinners and to set us free from the penalty of sin and death.

"But God showed his great love for us by sending Christ to die for us while we were still sinners. And since we have been made right in God's sight by the blood of Christ, he will certainly save us from God's judgment."

Romans 5:8-9 (NLT)

God has provided a way for you to be made right with Him through Christ.

"For God made Christ, who never sinned, to be the offering for our sin, so that we could be made right with God through Christ."

2 Corinthians 5:21 (NLT)

The only way to be made right with God is through Jesus Christ. It is essential that you understand and believe that there is nothing you can do to save yourself. The Word of God says:

> *"...the sinful mind is hostile to God. It does not submit to God's law, nor can it do so. Those controlled by the sinful nature cannot please God."*
>
> Romans 8:7-8 (NIV)

Without Christ it is impossible to submit to God or obey Him.

> *"Once you were dead, doomed forever because of your many sins. You used to live just like the rest of the world, full of sin, obeying Satan, the mighty prince of the power of the air. He is the spirit at work in the hearts of those who refuse to obey God. All of us used to live that way, following the passions and desires of our evil nature. We were born with an evil nature, and we were under God's anger just like everyone else. But God is so rich in mercy, and he loved us so very much, that even while we were dead because of our sins, **he gave us life** when he raised Christ from the dead. (**It is only by God's special favor [grace] that you have been saved!**)"*
>
> Ephesians 2:1-5 (NLT; emphasis added)

> *"God saved you by his special favor (grace) when you believed. And you can't take credit for this; it is a gift from God. Salvation is not a reward for the good things we have done, so none of us can boast about it."*
>
> Ephesians 2:8-9 (NLT)

> *"Create in me a clean heart, O God. Renew a right spirit within me."*
>
> Psalm 51:10

> *"He saved us, not because of the good things we did, but because of his mercy. He washed away our sins and gave us a new life through the Holy Spirit. He generously poured out the Spirit upon us because of what Jesus Christ our Savior did. He declared us not guilty [justification] because of his great kindness. And now we know that we will inherit eternal life."*
>
> Titus 3:5-7 (NLT)

Salvation is a gift of God that a person receives by faith. You must believe that you are a sinner in need of salvation—there is no way to save yourself from the penalty of your sin—and you must believe that Jesus Christ came to pay the penalty for sin by giving His life for you on the cross.

> *"For Christ died for sins once for all, the righteous for the unrighteous, to bring you to God. He was put to death in the body but made alive by the Spirit."*
>
> 1 Peter 3:18 (NIV)

Do you see your need for the Savior? There is much confusion about how a person gets saved or redeemed due to the influence of evangelistic methods that promote praying a prayer or asking Jesus into your heart.

There is no prayer that saves you. There is no special formula to receive Christ. What is necessary is a biblical response to the Gospel. You must understand that you are a sinner in need of salvation and that you cannot save yourself by any works or deeds. You must believe by faith that Jesus Christ came to be your Savior and that He died on the cross for your sins and accept His free gift of salvation.

You have been divinely enabled to believe and respond to the gospel by God and in that first moment of belief several amazing things take place.

You are justified in Christ. You are adopted as a child of God. You are set apart (sanctified) and made righteous before God. You also gain access to the throne room of God because you are no longer an enemy who is under His wrath, but His beloved child.

He also comes to dwell within you in the person of the Holy Spirit and you are changed forever.

He removes your heart of stone and gives you a heart of flesh that is able to be transformed and conformed to the image and likeness of Christ.

If you want to pray a prayer, there is of course no harm in talking to God about what He has done for you in Christ.

Many people are moved to confession of sin and repentance as a part of what God is supernaturally doing within them. It is critical you understand it is faith—not a prayer—that saves you.

Salvation in Jesus Christ is what brings the ability for heart change.

Once saved, you have now been enabled to change on the heart level (mind, thoughts, desires, intentions, emotions) through the Person of Christ and the power of the Holy Spirit living His life in you. The Lord empowers you to make the changes in your heart that are evidenced in your behavior.

The changes you must make may not be easy.

In some cases you will be changing sinful behaviors and habits you have had for most of your life. The good news is that change is possible!

> *"His divine power has given us **everything** we need for life and godliness through our knowledge of him who called us by his own glory and goodness. Through these he has given us his very great and precious promises, so that through them you may participate in the divine nature and escape the corruption in the world caused by evil desires."*
> 2 Peter 1:3-4 (NIV; emphasis added)

Repentance

There are many questions regarding repentance and how to know when a person has truly repented. Repentance is critical in overcoming any kind of sin.

Biblically, true repentance is a threefold response to sin that is found in the use of three different words that express different aspects of repentance. All three components must be present for there to be fruit of true repentance in a person's life.

The first response of repentance is found in the Greek word metanoeo which means a "change of mind" (Matt. 3:2, Mark 1:15).

When a person has a change of mind it means that there has been acknowledgment of sin. This is what we find when a person confesses their sin. They admit and understand that what they have done is sinful. There is no justification or rationalization attached to the sin, no attempts to minimize or blame shift the responsibility for it onto someone else. There is personal guilt attached to the acts that have been committed.

Repentance cannot stop here because it is incomplete. There are plenty of situations where a person has confessed sin and admitted their guilt and nothing more happens. There is no other visible change and things go back to normal; meaning the sin resumes at some point or something else takes its place.

An excellent example of this would be the Pharaoh as he dealt with Moses and the Israelites. Twice (Ex. 9:27; 10:16) he admitted to Moses, "I have sinned against the Lord your God." He admitted he sinned, he did not justify or rationalize or shift the blame and yet he did not repent. There were no changes that accompanied his admission; in fact, he went right back to his behavior!

King Saul had the same kind of limited repentance (1 Sam. 15:24, 24:17; 26:21) and he did not cease in pursuing David no matter how sorry he was. It is clear that just admitting sin does not equal repentance.

The second critical aspect of repentance is metanolomai (Matt. 21:29, 32; Heb. 7:21) and it means "change of heart." In addition to admitting and confessing sin there must be a change of heart with respect to the sin; what a person once loved and worshiped is now hated.

There is no longer room in the heart for fulfilling various lusts; in fact there is a growing hatred for everything that leads to that particular sin in the first place. We could call this a holy hatred and it is an emotional response that is experienced in the body in the form of deep sorrow over their sin.

Worldly Sorrow/Godly Sorrow

An important difference must be made here: there is a great difference between worldly sorrow and godly sorrow. Godly sorrow has as its first concern the honor of God. It is others oriented and is produced by the Holy Spirit acting on the conscience of a sinner. This kind of sorrow cries out, "Woe is me!" and causes a person to weep bitterly over the sin that has been committed.

When the Apostle Peter denied Christ three times after the arrest of Jesus, he went off and wept (metanoeo). He was heartbroken over his sin and over how he had betrayed the One he loved. By comparison Judas also repented (metamelo-mai), meaning he had a change of heart about betraying an innocent man. He felt guilty about it and sought to rectify it by returning the money he was paid. His hope was to erase his guilt and somehow undo what he had done. He then went and hung himself (Matthew 27:3-5).

It is important to note that repentance is a manifestation of the life of Christ in a person. It is a proof of salvation in a person's life. The sinner (Peter in the above example) has been cut deeply to the heart by the Spirit of God and or the Word of God and understands that his sin is grievous to the Lord. Because he accepted and understood that spiritual reality, he no longer desired to participate in it.

Worldly sorrow is "unsanctified remorse"[1] (Judas in the above example) and is focused on feelings of regret, fear, and even desperation. The person's focus is on how the sin or its exposure will affect him. MacArthur further says that worldly sorrow "has no redemptive capability. It is nothing more than the wounded pride of getting caught in a sin and having one's lusts go unfulfilled." [2]

The first two kinds of repentance take place in the inner man, or the heart. This is critical because as the heart changes, the actions change. This leads us to the third part of this critical aspect of change.

Finally, there must be metanoia which is a "change the course of life" (Matthew 3:8; 9:13; Acts 20:21). We know that the apostle Peter truly did repent because his life demonstrated all of the aspects of repentance: he understood his sin (fear), he grieved over his sin (fear of man), and his life changed (he boldly proclaimed Christ for the rest of his life, ultimately being martyred for the faith).

Changing the course of life involves an act of the will, a turning from the sinful behavior. There must be a radical amputation of the actions.

> *"If your hand causes you to stumble, cut it off; it is better for you to enter life crippled, than, having your two hands, to go into hell, into the unquenchable fire,[where their worm does not die, and the fire is not quenched.] "If your foot causes you to stumble, cut it off; it is better for you to enter life lame, than, having your two feet, to be cast into hell, [where their worm does not die, and the fire is not quenched.] "If your eye causes you to stumble, throw it out; it is better for you to enter the kingdom of God with one eye, than, having two eyes, to be cast into hell.* Mark 9:43-47

When repentance is genuine you will see all of this and the change will be dramatic.

Repentance is not something a person can conjure up from within. No amount of screaming or threatening or other forms of manipulation will force a person to repent. Repentance is a gift from God. Repentance can come quickly or sometimes will take years but one thing is certain: A regenerated Christian will repent. There will be no way for him/her to live under the conviction and ministry of the Holy Spirit without repenting.

1John MacArthur Study Bible footnotes on 1 Corinthians 7:10
2Ibid

There must be a desire to change to glorify God before the changes will be biblical

You have been divinely enabled to change, to be holy, to live the life God has called you to live! I hope this causes you to shout, "Praise the Lord!"

Often when counselees come with a problem, their goal in counseling is to feel better. They mistakenly believe that if they exit counseling feeling better, it has been successful. When this is the motive, all too often the problems that brought them to counseling reappear and their sorrow deepens to hopelessness. This is because the goal of the counseling is off base.

The goal of all counseling is change, but not change in circumstances or change in feelings. The goal of biblical counseling is heart-level change that brings about a life that glorifies God.

This means God's priorities become your priorities. What He says in His Word is important to Him and becomes important to you.

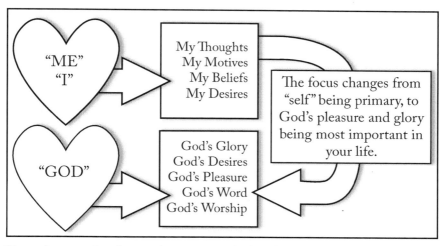

These changes take place in the inner man before they are evidenced in behavior.

III Inner Man Inner Life

The Bible has plenty to say about the workings of the inner man and the resulting behavior. I would like you to focus on a few key passages to aid you in understanding the process of biblical change.

The first is that we are commanded to change.

> *"With the Lord's authority let me say this: Live no longer as the Gentiles do, for they are hopelessly confused."* Ephesians 4:17 (NLT)

> *"Do not let sin control the way you live; do not give in to its lustful desires. Do not let any part of your body become a tool of wickedness, to be used for sinning. Instead, give yourselves completely to God since you have been given new life. And use your whole body as a tool to do what is right for the glory of God."* Romans 6:12-13 (TLB)

> *"Therefore, I urge you, brothers, in view of God's mercy, to offer your bodies as living sacrifices, holy and pleasing to God—this is your spiritual act of worship. Do not conform any longer to the pattern of this world, but be transformed by the renewing of your mind."* Romans 12:1-2 (NIV)

The renewing of the mind spoken of in Romans 12:2 is one aspect of heart change. To be "transformed" is the Greek word *metamorphoo* that we translate metamorphosis. It means: to transform (literally or figuratively "metamorphose") —change, transfigure, transform. It is most often compared to the caterpillar transforming into the butterfly.

Your heart was transformed at salvation from a heart of stone that hated God to one that is a heart of flesh that is capable of loving God (Ezekiel 36:26) and serving and worshipping Him.

Just as the butterfly in no way resembles the caterpillar, you are no longer to be fashioned like/shaped like, or resemble outwardly, the world's values, morals, behaviors, and beliefs.

> *"For though your hearts were once full of darkness, now you are full of light from the Lord, and your behavior should show it! For this light within you produces only what is good and right and true."*
> Ephesians 5:8-9 (TLB)

This kind of mind change only comes as the Holy Spirit changes your thinking through consistent study and meditation on the Word of God. This kind of study will enable you to know what God's will is for you.

"Don't copy the behavior and customs of this world, but let God transform you into a new person by changing the way you think. Then you will know what God wants you to do, and you will know how good and pleasing and perfect his will really is."
Romans 12:2 (NLT)

There is no better passage for describing the changes we are to undergo than what we find beginning in Ephesians 4:22:

"...throw off your old evil nature and your former way of life, which is rotten through and through, full of lust and deception. Instead, there must be a spiritual renewal of your thoughts and attitudes. You must display a new nature because you are a new person, created in God's likeness—righteous, holy, and true."
Ephesians 4:22-24 (NLT)

The New King James Version says it this way:

"...that you put off, concerning your former conduct, the old man which grows corrupt according to the deceitful lusts, and be renewed in the spirit of your mind, and that you put on the new man which was created according to God, in true righteousness and holiness."
Ephesians 4:22-24 (NKJV).

What are we to put off?

Selfish ambition: thinking of yourself before other people
Dissentions: causing trouble
Factions: causing divisions
Envy: wanting what someone else has
Drunkenness: alcoholism, drinking to excess
Orgies: group sex
Unrighteousness: injustice, or iniquity in general
Wickedness: a desire to injure others; malice; striving to cause injury to others
Covetousness: the desire to obtain what belongs to others
Licentiousness: evil in general; the act of doing wrong rather than the desire which is expressed by the word "wickedness"
Murder: the unlawful taking of a human life, usually thought out beforehand with a desire to see others suffer.
Debate: contention, strife, altercation, connected with anger and heated zeal. (This contention and strife would, of course, follow from malice and covetousness, etc.)
Deceit: This denotes fraud, falsehood.
Malignity: misinterpreting the words or actions of others, or putting the worst construction on their conduct
Whisperers: gossipers; those who secretly and in a sly manner, by hints and innuendoes, detract from others
Wraths: anger or animosities between contending factions, the usual effect of forming parties

Strife: between contending factions

Factions: split up into parties who are embittered and resentful of on another with mutual blaming and accusations, as they are in a church

Backbiters: those who slander or speak ill of those who are absent

Haters of God

Despiteful: This word denotes those who abuse or treat others with unkindness or disdain.

Proud: Pride is well understood. It is an inordinate self-esteem; an unreasonable conceit of one's superiority in talents, beauty, wealth, accomplishments, etc. (Webster's)

Boasters: those who speak of themselves in a self-admiring way, or demand or seize qualities they do not possess and glory in it. This is closely related to pride.

Inventors of evil things: seeking to find out new arts or plans to practice evil; new devices to gratify lusts and passions; new forms of luxury, and vice, etc.

Disobedient to parents: This expresses the idea that they did not show to parents honor, respect, and attention which was due.

Without understanding: inconsiderate or foolish

Covenant breakers: false to their contracts

Without natural affections: This expression denotes a lack of affectionate regard toward their children. Refers here to the practice of exposing their children, or putting them to death—abortion, infanticide.

Unmerciful: destitute of compassion

Unrighteous: the unjust; those who do injustice to others, attempting to do it under the sanction of the courts

Effeminate: applied to morals; as it is here, it denotes those who make self-indulgence the grand object of life, those who are given up to wantonness and sensual pleasures, or who are kept to be prostituted to others

Revilers: coarse, harsh, and bitter words; those who are characterized by abusing others, vilifying their character and wounding their feelings

Thieves: extortionists, persons greedy of gain, who oppress the poor, the needy, and the fatherless, to obtain money

Rioting: Reveling; denoting behavior that lacks morality and is sexual in conduct, noisy and defiant partying, scenes of disorder and sensuality, which attend luxurious living.

Drunkenness: rioting and drunkenness

Lewd, immodest behavior: includes illicit indulgences of all kinds, adultery, etc.

Strife: envying contention, disputes, litigation

Envying: any intense, vehement, "fervid" passion.

*You will find these listed in Galatians 5:19, Romans 1:24-32;13:13; 1 Corinthians 6:9-10; Colossians 3:5.

Do you have any of these sins in your life?

You may struggle with some or many of these sins today, even though you are a Christian. You will never be completely free from all sin while on earth, but by

God's grace as you grow in Christ, you will see a decrease in your sinful habits and an increase in righteous thinking and behavior.

The second version of Ephesians 4:22 tells us that the old man "grows corrupt" according to the deceitful lusts. Our flesh (old man, sinful nature) will be with us until the day we leave this earth.

If it is fed, it will continue to flourish and grow stronger and more corrupt. The flesh is not fed by goodness; it is fed by sinful thoughts and desires that lead to sinful actions. Its desires are insatiable.

An excellent illustration of corruption comes from ancient Roman justice. When a man committed murder, one method of punishment was to strap the dead body of the victim to the murderer. The victim would be tied to the murderer at the wrists, chest, legs, and ankles to give maximum skin contact. The murderer would have to carry his victim everywhere he went; there was no escape. As the body of the victim began to decompose, flies would gather and maggots would soon cover the body. Acid from the decomposition would begin to eat into the skin of the murderer, opening him up to infection from the flies and other means. The stench from the rotting flesh would nauseate the host, and he would beg for release from this torture. He would want more than anything to be able to throw off this rotting, stinking corpse and get away. Eventually the murderer would die of septic shock, blood poisoning, or another infection.

The illustration points out that the flesh grew more and more corrupt as it stayed in contact with the rotting flesh to the point that it snuffed the life out of the host.

> *"For if you live according to the sinful nature, you will die; but if by the Spirit you put to death the misdeeds of the body, you will live."*
>
> Romans 8:13 (ESV)

Bringing this back to you today, the longer you stay in contact with your former way of life and the sin it contained the more corrupt you will become. You are told to "put off," "throw off" your former conduct. This implies stripping off or flinging it far away from you as though it were that rotting corpse.

In addition to putting off the old man, you must be renewed in the spirit of your mind.

> *"Instead, there must be a spiritual renewal of your thoughts and attitudes."*
>
> Ephesians 4:23 (NLT)

The Word and Spirit supply what is needed to renew your mind (Rom 12:1-2). This is inseparably coupled with changed living and enables you to understand, believe and obey.

> *"...you have stripped off your old evil nature and all its wicked deeds. In its place you have clothed yourselves with a brand-new nature that is continually*

being renewed as you learn more and more about Christ, who created this new nature within you."   Colossians 3:9b-10 (NKJV)

When you became a Christian, God gave you a completely new spiritual and moral capacity that a mind apart from Christ could never achieve (1 Corinthians 2:9-16). Your mind is the center of thought, understanding, belief, desire, and motivation. This is why it is critical to begin to renew your mind with His Word.

It is not adequate just to change your behavior, because what drives the behavior is still the same. Your mind must be retrained to operate biblically so that when you are presented with the same old temptations, you think a new response. Instead of, "If I tell the truth, I am going to be in trouble," the new thought will become, "Telling the truth is the way I will honor God, even if it means I am disciplined. It is more important to be honest than it is to look good or escape being disciplined."

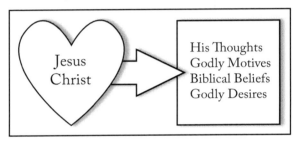

You cannot assume that only new thinking will lead to walking worthy/ new living. You must also deal with what is standing in your way of belief and action. Genuine change is more than stopping wrong behavior. There must be repentance that includes an understanding that the actions are not glorifying to God. There must be a change in the manner of life that you live. Genuine repentance is accompanied by a desire to obey. You cannot separate thinking from obedience.

> *"And remember, it is a message to obey, not just to listen to. If you don't obey, you are only fooling yourself. For if you just listen and don't obey, it is like looking at your face in a mirror but doing nothing to improve your appearance. You see yourself, walk away, and forget what you look like."*
> James 1:22-24 (NLT)

When Jesus Christ is the ruler of your heart (inner man), your thoughts, understanding, beliefs, desires, and motivations flow from what He wants you to do as seen in His Word.

> *"Finally, You must display a new nature* [put on the new self, put on the new man] *because you are a new person, created in God's likeness—righteous, holy, and true."*
> Ephesians 4:24 (NLT; verse quoted with my additions)

This indicates a change of your entire lifestyle. Real change begins in the heart and flows out through your life to reflect Christ in you.

22

Some specific examples of putting off/putting on from Ephesians 4 & 5:

PUT OFF	PUT ON
• 4:25 Put away lying	• Speak truth
• 4:26 Do not sin in your anger	• Don't carry anger overnight; forgive
• 4:28 Stop stealing	• Work for what you need so you can share with others
• 4:9 Stop corrupt speech	• Say things that build others up and give grace to the hearer
• 4:31 Put away all bitterness, wrath, anger, loud quarreling, evil speaking	• Be kind to others, tenderhearted, forgiving, imitators of God; walk in love, giving thanks
• 5:3 Fornication, uncleanness, Covetousness	• 5:11 Have no fellowship with the deeds of unrighteousness
• 5:4 Filthiness, foolish talk, coarse jesting	• 5:15 Walk carefully, wisely, understanding what God's will is.
• Manifest the deeds of the flesh	• Manifest the fruit of the Spirit

"Don't be fooled by those who try to excuse these sins, for the terrible anger of God comes upon all those who disobey him. Don't participate in the things these people do. For though your hearts were once full of darkness, now you are full of light from the Lord, and your behavior should show it! For this light within you produces only what is good and right and true. Try to find out what is pleasing to the Lord. Take no part in the worthless deeds of evil and darkness; instead, rebuke and expose them. It is shameful even to talk about the things that ungodly people do in secret."

Ephesians 5:6-12 (NLT)

All these changes are possible and required by God. He never tells us *what* to do without telling *how* to do it or *equipping* us to do it.

"Now to him who is able to do immeasurably more than all we ask or imagine, according to his power that is at work within us."

Ephesians 3:20 (NIV)

"I am the true vine, and my Father is the gardener. He cuts off every branch that doesn't produce fruit, and he prunes the branches that do bear fruit so they will produce even more. You have already been pruned for greater fruitfulness

by the message I have given you. Remain in me, and I will remain in you. For a branch cannot produce fruit if it is severed from the vine, and you cannot be fruitful apart from me. Yes, I am the vine; you are the branches. Those who remain in me, and I in them, will produce much fruit. For apart from me you can do nothing."
John 15:1-5 (NLT)

"For God is working in you, giving you the desire to obey him and the power to do what pleases him."
Philippians 2:13 (NLT)

Heart change is done by the Spirit of God. The process of sanctification is evidence of your salvation. Were it not for the Holy Spirit living inside you, you would have no desire to change your heart or to glorify God.

God is pleased with you because of Christ, and that does not change. His pleasure rests upon you because His wrath has been satisfied for the sake of Christ.

The "pleasing" of God that is done in the sanctification process is glorifying to His name and Person. It is contained in revealing Christ in you to others, introducing them to the character and Person of Christ through you. This brings God much glory.

IV Change is a battle for the mind that is fought in the body

I am frequently asked for some practical ways to change. These are some biblical suggestions:

Think about your thoughts.
Ask yourself if your thoughts, words, actions, or desires are glorifying to God *before* you do them.

Memorize Scripture.
Memorize Scripture that specifically relates to the sin that you struggle with.

Be honest with God.
> *"Search me, O God, and know my heart; test me and know my thoughts. Point out anything in me that offends you, and lead me along the path of everlasting life."*
> Psalm 139:23-24

God is all-knowing and knows what is in your heart before you do. He is acquainted with all your ways.

> *"O LORD, you have examined my heart and know everything about me. You know when I sit down or stand up. You know my every thought when far away. You chart the path ahead of me and tell me where to stop and rest. Every moment you know where I am. You know what I am going to say even before I say it, LORD."*
> Psalm 139:1-4

This request is a sign of humility and submission to who He is. To ask God to see if there is any wickedness in you indicates your desire to change.

Confess your sin to God.
> *"If we say we have no sin, we are only fooling ourselves and refusing to accept the truth. But if we confess our sins to him, he is faithful and just to forgive us and to cleanse us from every wrong."*
> 1 John 1:8-9 (NLT)

Admitting your sin is a sign of the Holy Spirit working within you. Confession is agreeing with God that what you have done is wrong and is offensive to Him. When you know you have done wrong, you are responsible to change your behavior through the renewing of your mind.

Keep a thought journal.

This has proven to be an effective tool in the process of biblical change. Write down what you are thinking, believing and desiring in your heart throughout the day, especially at times that you sin. Afterward, review the journal and see if you can support your thoughts, beliefs, or desires biblically. See if you can find Scripture that contextually supports you or Scripture that reveals to you that you were wrong and sinned. Confess your sin to God, thank him for His forgiveness, and seek to memorize the verses that pertain to your specific sinful struggles.

Take every thought captive.

> *"We demolish arguments and every pretension that sets itself up against the knowledge of God, and we take captive every thought to make it obedient to Christ."*   2 Corinthians 10:5

Remember that what you think in your heart is what drives your behavior. When you are beginning this process of mind renewal, there are many more old thought patterns to battle. You cannot conquer your thought life with traditional weapons. Your battle takes place in the unseen world of your mind and heart.

While turning off the TV or leaving corrupting company is a tangible way to do battle, the bulk of this war —and it is a war— is internal. You must assault your old, sinful thought patterns with the truth of God's Word. You must capture these thoughts and subject them to biblical scrutiny. Do they pass the test of heart change? Do they past the test of glorifying God? The above verse says you must "demolish arguments [thoughts, ideas, speculations, reasoning's, philosophies, and false religions] and every pretension that sets itself up [exalts itself] against the knowledge of God" (amplification added).

This is a battle that takes place in the mind—and you can expect a battle! You may have been living with sinful thought patterns for many years. Is it reasonable to expect to change all of them rapidly? Indeed, some change may come easily; but some of your behaviors, thoughts, and desires will not be so easily changed.

> *"The old sinful nature loves to do evil, which is just opposite from what the Holy Spirit wants. And the Spirit gives us desires that are opposite from what the sinful nature desires. These two forces are constantly fighting each other, and your choices are never free from this conflict."*
>   Galatians 5:17 (NLT)

These two natures are at war with each other; they desire opposite things. The flesh will lead you toward sinful behavior. The Spirit will remind you of what is right and what God desires—obedience that glorifies Him.

This will be an ongoing war until you reach glory.

Habits can be broken

Since these are sin habits, they can be changed. Thank God that these are not illnesses, defects, or disorders. What you struggle with is sin. Sin is serious, but not insurmountable! Your sin is serious enough that Jesus Christ died for it and gave you victory over it. You do not have to live your life in slavery to your current sinful thoughts, beliefs, and desires any longer.

> *"But remember that the temptations that come into your life are no different from what others experience. And God is faithful. He will keep the temptation from becoming so strong that you can't stand up against it. When you are tempted, he will show you a way out so that you will not give in to it."*
>
> 1 Corinthians 10:13 (NLT)

The times you do fail to take the way of escape and fall back into the sinful habit you are putting off, remember that change takes time and this is a process. You didn't develop this habit overnight and you may not conquer it overnight either.

Take heart

Wherever you find yourself in this change process, please be assured that you are exactly where God wants you to be. God is never surprised at your sin or your struggles with it. He never wastes anything, even our failures.

> *"And we know that God causes everything to work together for the good of those who love God and are called **according to his purpose for them**. For God knew his people in advance, and **he chose them to become like his Son**, so that his Son would be the firstborn, with many brothers and sisters. And having chosen them, he called them to come to him. And he gave them right standing with himself, and he promised them his glory."*
>
> Romans 8:28-30 (NLT; emphasis added)

All of these things are a part of what God is doing in and through you.

Be encouraged! Jesus Christ has provided the victory for you! The victory is yours for the taking! Because of who you are in Christ, you have the ability to change, and even greater than that, you have the God of the universe assisting you, caring for you, loving you. This should bring you tremendous hope!

By the power of God there is nothing that cannot be changed!

> *"Now to him who is able to do immeasurably* [exceedingly, abundantly, infinitely] *more than all we ask or imagine, according to his power that is at work within us, May he be given glory in the church and in Christ Jesus forever and ever through endless ages. Amen."*
>
> Ephesians 3:20-21 (amplifications added)

The Process of Biblical Change Homework Assignment

Contributed by Gaila Roper, Bill Schlacks, Sherrie Holman, Suzanne Holland & Julie Ganschow

Note: You will need 30-60 minutes *per day* to complete this homework over the next 1-2 weeks. This assignment is not intended to be rushed through, or to be completed thoughtlessly. The more thought and prayer you devote to completing this assignment, the more you will benefit from it.

Using your booklet and the Bible, complete the following study in a computer document to upload and email to your biblical counselor prior to your next session. Many of the answers to the questions in this study are found right in the booklet. Make note of any question you do not understand to discuss with your counselor.

What is the process of biblical change?

In short, we call this process *sanctification*. The initial sanctifying change occurs at salvation thru Christ's substitutionary work on the cross (2 Cor. 5:21). The change process continues, even after salvation, for the purpose of leaving behind who we were and advancing ahead. All the while, we are revealing the image of Christ in us, for the sole purpose of glorifying God (Phil.3:12-14). This ongoing aspect of change is called *progressive sanctification*.

Progressive sanctification is the process that is the will of God for us while we are here on earth (I Thess.4:3). It requires effort and perseverance to work out what God has already worked in you (2 Peter 1:3-4, Phil. 2: 12-13). Through progressive sanctification, we battle corruption from within and without, while seeking to honor Him in our lives.

True change must come at a heart level, affecting not only behavior but also character. This power to be and to do is the life of Christ working in and through us. It is not a form of godliness, or a powerless, legalistic conviction to do better. It is Him. We live for Him. He is worthy to receive all the honor and glory for this process.

To get you started, answer the following questions about yourself.

1. How have you trained yourself to respond to problems that you face in life?
2. Automatic behaviors are those we do without thinking. (An example would be driving from home to work while thinking about something else.) Those seeking counsel have often developed automatic behaviors that are problematic. What automatic behaviors do you know you struggle with? Write them below.

I. Change requires an understanding of your present heart condition.

A. Define the heart biblically.
    1. How many basic "parts" are you made of?
    2. At what times do you especially become aware of the immaterial part of you?

B. Bible Work
    1. What does Proverbs 4:27 say about behavior?
    2. What do Proverbs 15:15, 30 say about feelings?
    3. What does Proverbs 28:14 say about attitudes?

C. As you look at your own life in comparison with the above passages, examine your actions over the past week. Have you struggled with evil thoughts, bitterness, immorality, lying, or gossip?

D. Look up James 1:22-25. What does the passage say about the man who hears the Word but fails to act upon the Word?

E. Read Luke 6:45 and Matthew 15:18-19. Think about your own behaviors in light of what you've read.
    1. What do these verses tell you about the <u>origin</u> of your actions?
    2. What do these two passages of Scripture tell you about the importance of the heart?
    3. Can you think of a time when you have been counseled to "follow your heart?" What was the particular issue? Did you follow the counsel and what was the outcome?

F. Read Jeremiah 17:9
    1. What does the Bible say about the condition of your heart?
    2. According to this verse, is your heart trustworthy?
    3. Do you think that one aspect of Christian growth might include an increasing sensitivity to the state of your heart?
    4. Since the heart is the control center that guides and determines your actions, what generates your behavior? (See the diagram [page 6] on the heart.)
    5. Looking at that same diagram, how much of what you are struggling with is centered on your belief that, "I must satisfy 'me', I must have my own way, or live life for my pleasures?"

G. The Importance of Roots/Fruits
For this section, please refer to the tree diagram on pages 8 and 9 in the booklet. The trees on pages 8-9 contain some, but not all the fruit that a person may be producing. No one produces "all bad" or "all good" fruit, most of us produce a mixture of good and bad fruit in our lives.

1. What "fruit" do you see in your own life? Is it good fruit or poor fruit? List them.
2. What does your fruit (behavior/responses) reveal about the condition of your heart?
3. Have you previously tried to "make" good fruit appear in your life?
4. What methods did you use?
5. How successful were your attempts?
6. How long did it take you to revert back to your old behaviors?
7. You have learned that the heart is the control center containing and producing your thoughts, beliefs, motives, and desires.

  a. Draw your own tree, including the fruit of your behavior on top and the possible root causes in the ground. Write on the trunk of the tree what you think motivates you to act in this way. This will be harder--hang in there! Remember, all of your actions, including whatever it was that brought you to counseling, began as a thought, belief, or desire in your heart.

  b. Can you see the connection between the desire of your heart (roots) and the behavior (fruit) you are experiencing?

  c. Who or what are you focused on?

  d. Who do you desire to please?

  e. What is more important that your happiness?

  f. Have you tried in the past just to stop wrong or bad behaviors with little success?

  g. With this in mind, write a couple of paragraphs explaining your understanding of the relationship between the root and fruit in your life.

8. Only God can change the human heart (hope is established). Write a couple of paragraphs with Scriptures on what God has done and is doing to accomplish change in your heart.

9. A new heart is given by God at salvation. Salvation is necessary because of sin.

  a. What have you been taught over the years? Is man basically good or basically bad? What Scriptures would you cite to support your answer?

  b. Read Hebrews 11:1. How do you assess your own assurance of your salvation? Do you assess your assurance on the basis of emotions (how you feel), personal experience or on the promises of God?

  c. What do John 5:24, 11:25-26 promise?

  d. What would it mean in your daily life to fully embrace God's plan of redemption?

  e. Without Christ it is **impossible** to submit to God or obey Him. Write a paragraph about why you believe this is or is not true.

  f. Salvation in Jesus Christ is what brings the ability for heart change.

  g. Can you explain what God has done for you in salvation?

  h. How has your life changed since your salvation?

  i. The changes you must make may not be easy!

Look up 2 Peter 1:3-4. Write out a paragraph below on how this passage is true about the problems you are facing today.

10. 2 Corinthians 7:10 speaks of 2 different forms of repentance.

    a. What is "worldly repentance?"

    b. What is repentance unto salvation?

    c. When have you experienced sorrow over a sin but not truly repented of it?

    d. Explain why merely recognizing and confessing sin is not enough to accomplish true repentance.

    e. Explain why worldly sorrow is referred to as "unsanctified remorse."

    f. Read Luke 3:8-14. What do you think the "fruit in keeping with repentance" is?

    g. Do you think it is possible for someone to genuinely trust in Christ for forgiveness of their sins without also sincerely repenting of their sins?

    h. As you study this verse, write a paragraph about your understanding of what it will mean for you to truly repent.

II. There must be a desire to change to glorify God before the changes will be biblical.

A. The Westminster Confession states "Man's chief end is to glorify God, and enjoy Him forever. Did you come to biblical counseling with different goals in mind?

    1. Re-read the text and examine the diagram on page 17. What must change if you are to bring glory to God by how you live your life?

    2. Read 1 Thessalonians 4:3. What is God's will for you? Did you come to counseling with different goals in mind?

III. Inner Man/Inner Life

A. The Command to Change

    1. What does "transformed" mean?

    2. Respond in paragraph form to this question: "What aspect of your heart and mind need to be transformed?"

    3. Using Scriptures in this section of the booklet, write a couple of paragraphs detailing the process of renewing the mind.

    4. Study the "put off" list on pages 19 and 20 in your booklet (Scriptures: Gal. 5:19; Rom. 1:24-32, 13:13; I Cor. 6:9-10; Col. 3:5).

        a. Do you see any of the sins listed there in yourself?

        b. Which ones are new to you?

        c. With which of these sins have you been known to struggle?

        d. What have you done in the past to try and deal with these sins?

    5. In light of what you have learned through completing your homework,

what kind of a heart has generated these sins? Go back to your tree, if needed.

We know that you will never be completely free from all sin while on earth, but by God's grace as you grow in Christ, you will see a decrease in your sinful habits and an increase in righteous thinking and behavior (see Eph. 4:22). Do you realize that these areas of sin do not glorify God?

B. The illustration of Roman justice often affects people as they think of their own sin being like a dead body they haul around as it eats into their flesh. As you look at the sin you know you must put off, write a paragraph or two of reaction to this illustration.

IV. Change is a battle for the mind that is fought in the body.

A. There are eight tools, or habits of discipline, that are maintenance related:

1. **Think about your thoughts**—ask yourself if your thoughts, words, actions, or desires are glorifying to God *before* you do them! I suggest making index cards that say, "Does this _____ glorify God?" and place them on your mirrors, books, dashboard, workspace, television or computer monitor. Literally, put them any place that you know you are prone to sin as a reminder of what you are trying to do. This has proven to be a very helpful tool in the early days of change to keep the mind focused in the right direction and to catch one's self in automatic behavior.

2. **Keep a Thought Journal.** Some people find it helpful to keep a Thought Journal to help them recognize unbiblical thoughts. Detailed Thought Journal instructions are found on page 26. Jot your thoughts, beliefs, and desires down on paper or use your electronic device to record your thoughts, beliefs, and desires when you're struggling. There is a great temptation to disregard the importance of the Thought Journal, but it is the single most useful exercise you will undertake in biblical counseling!

Initially, this may be a struggle for you. Typically, I receive resistance to keeping the journal, but I tell you it is one of the most effective tools for change. The objections for this activity tend to be along the lines of struggling with putting thoughts on paper, and this is exactly why it is so effective. Those who struggle with automatic behavior are not actively thinking, they are reacting to longstanding habits and behaviors.

I suggest writing down what you are thinking, believing, and desiring in your heart throughout the day, especially during times when you have sinned or want to sin. Then, review the journal and see if you can support your thoughts, beliefs, or desires biblically. The goal in this assignment is to help you see your thoughts in an objective manner. See if you can find Scripture that contextually supports your thoughts or reveals that you were wrong and sinned. Confess your sin to God, thank Him for His forgiveness, and seek to memorize the verses that speak to your specific sinful struggles to help you overcome them.

3. **Memorize Scripture** verses that specifically address the sin(s) you are struggling with. The Bible is powerful! You will not change apart from the inspired Word of God (Psalm 119:9-11). Writing out these applicable verses on cards and putting them together in a flip chart can be helpful. They are easily portable, fit in a pocket, purse, or book bag and can be used anywhere. Repetition is the most effective way to memorize, so frequent readings of these cards will be very helpful.

4. **Be honest with God**—look up Psalm 139:23-24. God is sovereign. He knows you. Consider doing a study on the Sovereignty of God.

5. **Confess your sin to God**—read 1 John 1:8-9. "When you know you have done wrong, you are responsible to change your behavior through the renewing of your mind." (Grow up! You do not need to continue to live as a victim of sin [Romans 6]. Replace those lies with the truth of God's word, and an obedient, submissive heart.)

6. **Take every thought captive.** Read 2 Corinthians 10:5. Remember, what you think in your heart is what drives your behavior! This is largely an internal zone you will be battling. When you are beginning the process of mind renewal, there are many old thought patterns to be battled with. You cannot conquer your thought-life with traditional weapons; your battle takes place in the unseen world of your mind and heart.

While turning off the TV or leaving corrupting company is a tangible way to do battle, the bulk of this war is internal. It is a war.

You must assault your old and sinful thought patterns with the truth of God's Word. You must capture these thoughts and subject them to biblical scrutiny. Do they pass the test of heart change? Do they pass the test of glorifying God? This is a battle that takes place in the mind– and you can expect a battle! You may have been living with sinful thought patterns for many years. Is it reasonable to expect your thoughts to rapidly change?

Indeed, some change may come easily; but, some of your behaviors, thoughts, and desires will not be so easily changed.

7. **Habits can be broken.** Since these are sinful habits, they can be changed. Thank God that these are not illnesses, defects, or disorders. What you struggle with is sin. Sin is serious, but not insurmountable! Your sin is serious enough that Jesus Christ died for it and gave you victory over it. You no

longer have to live your life in slavery to your current sinful thoughts, beliefs, and desires.

Memorize 1 Corinthians 10:13! There will be times when you fail to take the way of escape God has provided, and you fall back into the sinful habit you were trying to put off. Just remember that change takes time and this is a process. You didn't develop this habit overnight, and you may not conquer it overnight either. With consistent application of what you have learned, there will be steady and measurable progress.

8. **Take Heart....** God is sovereign, even in your struggles. Wherever you find yourself in this change process, please be assured that you are exactly where God wants you to be. God is never surprised at your sin or your struggles with it. He never wastes anything, even our failures. All of these things are a part of what God is doing in and through you.

Be encouraged! Jesus Christ has provided the victory for you! The victory is yours for the taking! Because of who you are in Christ, you have the ability to change, and even greater than that, you have the God of the universe assisting you, caring for you, and loving you. This should bring you tremendous hope! By the power of God, there is nothing that cannot be changed! Read and memorize Ephesians 3:20-21.

"Because of who you are in Christ, you have the ability to change, and even greater than that, you have the God of the universe assisting you, caring for you, loving you."

Quote by Julie Ganschow

About the author

Julie Ganschow describes it as a joy to be involved in caring for hurting souls looking for help, healing, and hope. She began offering biblical counseling to women in 1998 and is a certified Biblical Counselor with numerous organizations, including the Association of Certified Biblical Counselors (ACBC) and the International Association of Biblical Counselors (IABC). She is also on the Counsel Board of the Biblical Counseling Coalition.

Julie has had extensive training and education and is pursuing her PhD in Biblical Counseling. She is the Founder and Director of Reigning Grace Counseling Center (RGCC), in Kansas City, Missouri. Julie is the author of a daily blog and numerous books and materials on counseling related issues.

It is her passion to show everyone that God's Word contains all the answers to life's problems and is completely sufficient. She strongly believes that heart change is the key to life change.

Julie is happily married to her high school sweetheart, Larry. Their family continues to grow as their three sons have married and grandchildren are beginning to arrive!

Made in the USA
Coppell, TX
27 January 2023

11778913R00022